WHY EVERY TEENAGER NEEDS A PARROT

Tips for parenting 21st Century Teenagers

ALICIA DRUMMOND

Design Dominic Latham-Koenig
Illustrations Olivia Whitworth

Published by Let's Talk Ltd
North Barnes House, North Barnes Lane,
East Chiltington, East Sussex, UK BN7 3DU

www.lets-talk.uk.com

ISBN 978-0-9927074-1-5

Printed and bound in the United Kingdom

Contents

Chapter 1
A PARROT?

EVERY TEENAGER NEEDS A PARROT

I HAVE JUST DROPPED MY SEVENTEEN YEAR OLD DAUGHTER AT THE station where she will catch a train to a friend's house by which point she will be at least an hour and a half from home. A gaggle of girls will swap gossip, advice, dresses and makeup before piling into a car and driving twenty minutes to a party. There will definitely be boys and alcohol; there might be adult supervision and food; drugs will be less conspicuous but nonetheless available.

My solitary drive home gives me plenty of time to consider the myriad of things that could go wrong. Nightmare visions of stomach pumps and pile ups flash through my mind and I wish, oh how I wish, that I could be sitting on her shoulder, like a parrot, saying, "*do this; don't do that; drink this; don't drink that; are you serious?!*"

Sadly I cannot be her parrot dishing out safety tips and advice but, what I can do is help her to develop a sensible parrot of her own and that is the point of this book.

The common parental perception of 21st Century teenagers is that they are so connected and mobile; drugs are everywhere; vodka their drink of choice; festivals after GCSE's and parent-free holidays in Ibiza a rite of passage (if you don't know what a week there might involve watch an episode of "Sun, Sex and Suspicious Parents" but be warned it makes for pretty uncomfortable viewing). As 21st Century parents we may think that we are parenting in difficult times but teenagers, or at least our attitude towards them, have not changed much over the centuries. Shakespeare wrote in Act 3, Scene 3 of A Winter's Tale "*I would there were no age between ten and three and twenty, or that youth would sleep out the rest; for there is nothing in the between but getting wenches with child, wronging the ancientry, stealing, fighting*". If you agree with The Bard then the good news is that your youth may well sleep out many of these years.

Even further back in the annals of time in AD 1274, Peter the Hermit wrote,

"*The world is passing through troublous times. The young people of today think of nothing but themselves. They have no reverence for parents or old age. They are impatient of all restraint. They talk as if they knew everything, and what passes as wisdom for us is foolishness with them. As for the girls, they are forward, immodest and unladylike in speech, behaviour and dress."*

Was he in Brighton on Saturday night?

As this is a book for the parents of teenagers I presume that you have made it through the early years of child rearing and are either in, or about to enter, the years of adolescence. For many parents I meet in the Let's Talk Teens Workshops, entering the Teen Zone is like staring down the barrels of a gun. When asked why they have come along to the workshop here are some of the answers they have given,

"because my twins are only 11 but it feels like they have already become teenagers and I feel horribly ill prepared."

"because every time I open a newspaper there seems to be another story about the latest fad that could kill my teens and I don't know how to keep them safe."

and finally, my personal favourite:

"because I have totally screwed it up with the first three and I want to get it right this time!"

For some of us the transition from being the parent of a child to being the parent of a teenager happens overnight, for others it creeps up on us. Either way it will happen sooner or later and when it does it can feel like someone has whipped the rug from underneath you.

Suddenly the little treasures we knew and understood start rolling their eyes at us, disappearing into their bedrooms for hours on end, listening to music with graphic lyrics at volumes you can barely stand, wearing clothes you want to pull up or down, piercing parts of their bodies you don't even know the names of. They no longer want to dance around the sofa with you on a Friday night - in fact the idea of you dancing at all is SOOOO embarrassing.

They want to be with their friends and if they can't be with them physically they will be with them virtually. Darwin would have been fascinated to see how thumbs, once primarily used for gripping, are adapting to fly across the tiny keyboards of mobile phones. Can you work out someone's age by watching which digits they use to write a text message? Maybe. Over 50 - index finger. Over 40 - Index and middle fingers. Under 30 - thumbs! There is even a name for repetitive strain injury of the thumb caused by texting, Blackberry Thumb - it is rarely seen in the over 40's!

I digress but I think you get the picture. Our children will become teenagers and for many parents the task of guiding them through this stage can feel like a daunting one. However, take heart because with understanding and the right tools, parenting teenagers can be exciting, interesting and hugely enjoyable. I am not a thrill seeker but I love not quite knowing what is going to happen from one day to the next. I love their wit and humour, their passion and conviction. We can have interesting debates; they are as good, if not better than me at activities we both enjoy; they are courageous and loyal and their friends are fun. Watching them pass through adolescence is both heartening and heartbreaking. It is a roller coaster ride that I am thoroughly enjoying. There are the odd moments when the day they fly our nest cannot come fast enough but, in truth, I dread it.

Sometimes I feel overwhelmed by all that we need to teach them before they go. I beat myself up for doing an inadequate job but then I remember the words of one of my tutors who said, "THERE IS NO SUCH THING AS THE PERFECT PARENT AND AS A CHILD YOU WOULDN'T WANT ONE" and so this book is NOT an invitation to beat yourself up. Hold tight to the fact that, in my experience of working with hundreds of families, parents do the best that they can with the tools that they have. Our children need us to be good enough, not perfect. Take what you will from the anecdotes, tips and information on offer. The fact that you are reading this suggests that you are open to ideas which makes your family luckier than many.

I was recently asked to be on the panel of a large senior school parents forum. My fellow panel members were an internet safety consultant and a drugs and alcohol expert. We were each asked to speak for fifteen minutes followed by a Q & A session and I was second in line. As I waited to give my presentation on "Helping Teens to Manage Exam Stress" I listened to the internet safety consultant. His talk about the dangers young people face on line was factual and hard hitting - this was someone who had worked at the coal face of the industry and knew exactly how the online underworld worked. Living and working with teens I learn a lot about what they are up to on-line but, by the end of his fifteen minutes even I was feeling decidedly wobbly and many of the parents around me looked positively shell shocked. One part of me felt angry with the presenter for frightening his audience without offering any solutions whilst another part of me applauded him for providing a wake up call despite the inadequate time slot allotted to tackle such a momentous subject.

The uneasy feeling I experienced could have been attributed to performance anxiety but over the days that followed I found my thoughts returning again and again to his talk. I realised that it was the lack of any solutions or guidance for parents that really bothered me. A wake up call is not enough. Parents need a toolbox; a plan that gives them the confidence, understanding and strategies to guide their teenagers through both the on and off line challenges of adolescence. It needs to be an action plan that will remain relevant long after Facebook has had its heyday. A plan which recognizes that this generation was born into a digital world where much of what they are exposed to is alien to us and is constantly changing. A plan that recognizes that they are more mobile and connected than humans have ever been. A plan that is practical, positive and easy to apply.

My workshops often explore the pull that parents feel between letting their teenagers go and grow and keeping them safe. Striking the balance between the two can be extraordinarily difficult. I am a parent of teenagers, I work with teenagers in schools and in therapy and I work with parents and teachers. I am regularly exposed to the needs of all parties and I recognize that there is a very real and fine balancing act to be achieved. When our teenagers are faced with difficult or potentially dangerous situations, which, let's face it, rarely happens when we are in the vicinity, how reassuring would it be to be able to issue on the spot advice? And so we return to the parrot.

Baby parrots don't emerge from their shells able to speak English, Japanese or any other language but parrot. They learn the language and behavior that we repeatedly teach them and whilst they might not always use the right phrase at the right time, if we don't put anything in we won't get anything out. Developing your teenagers' parrot is about giving them information and skills that they can draw on in any given circumstance. It is about getting them to think as they are much more likely to sign up to an idea if they have invested in it in some way. Their parrot needs to be well informed and well rehearsed because it is that friendly voice of reason that will be all important when they are faced with difficult situations and choices. They won't always make the right decisions but a parrot who is well programmed and can speak with a loud and clear voice is much more difficult to ignore.

So, how do we go about programming their parrot? If you have ever watched the film The Horse Whisperer with Robert Redford you will know that the secret of training horses is to understand horse psychology and to work with their natural instincts. In the same way, if we understand the developmental drive of teenagers we can work with that drive rather than constantly banging up against it.

There are no guarantees but if the worst does happen and we have had the right conversations with them perhaps the "if only's" might not torment us for ever.

But stop, I am beginning to sound like Mr Internet Safety. I promised myself that this book would be a positive guide to help parents and teenagers to be successful in weathering the sometimes stormy waters of adolescence. Our job as parents is not only to keep them safe but to set them up to be adults who can go out into the world and communicate effectively with themselves and others; who are respectful of themselves and others; who can show empathy; who are self motivated; able to make decisions and take responsibility for those decisions; who are, in short, emotionally intelligent and, therefore, well placed to become the best adults they can be.

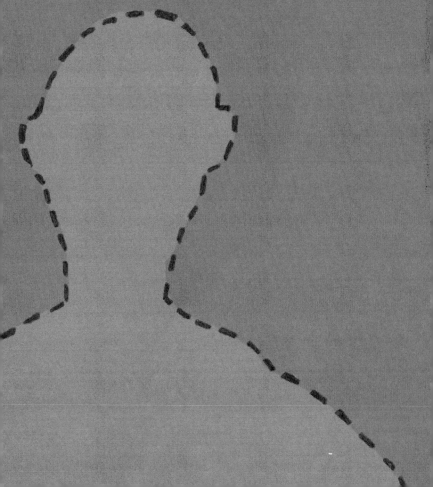

Chapter 2
WHAT'S GOING ON?

As parents we are largely responsible for our children's environment and if we can create one in which emotional intelligence is nurtured and strengthened then we give them the most fertile soil in which to grow. I am no gardener, but I do understand that different plants have different needs and will only flourish if those needs are met. Likewise, our children have different needs at different times in their development and we can only meet those needs if we understand their development.

I promise not to overload you with theory, but there are certain things that are important and the rest of this chapter covers one of them . If the idea of theory fills you with horror you have the choice to read it or not. Just don't be surprised if lots of other bits of the book don't make sense should you choose to skip straight to chapter three!

1950s Berlin is where it was all happening in the world of psychology and one of the most important figures of that era was psychologist Erik Erikson. As a follower of Freud, Erikson believed that what happens to us in childhood affects how we are as adults.

He developed a model of human personality development in which he proposed that in the course of our lifetime we pass through eight stages and each stage presents a challenge that needs to be overcome. If you look at the table opposite you will see that Erikson gives an age range for each stage followed by two outcomes. If our passage through each stage is successful then we acquire the belief shown in Column Three and if unsuccessful we acquire the opposing belief shown in Column Four.

Let's look at the childhood stages to give you a clearer idea of what Erikson was on about:

Stage 1 - Trust versus Mistrust

In this stage we are babies and totally reliant on our parents for our survival. If our needs are met with reasonable reliability ie when we are hungry we are fed; when we are wet we are changed and when we need a cuddle we get one, then we learn that people are basically trustworthy and we carry this belief through to adulthood. In other words we develop trust and

Stage	Age	Column 3	Column 4
Stage 1	0 - 2 years	Trust	Mistrust
Stage 2	2 - 5 years	Autonomy	Shame
Stage 3	5 - 7 years	Initiative	Guilt
Stage 4	7 - 12 years	Industry	Inferiority
Stage 5	12 - 20 years	Identity	Identity Diffusion
Stage 6	20 - 30 years	Intimacy	Isolation
Stage 7	30 - 65 years	Generativity	Self Absorption
Stage 8	65+ years	Integrity	Despair

hope that others will be there for us when we need them. If the care we receive during this stage is unreliable or inconsistent then we develop mistrust and it is hard for us to believe that others will be there for us when we need them.

Stage 2 - Autonomy versus Shame & Doubt

This stage represents our first quest for independence as we start to move and walk and explore the world around us. If a toddler's seeking and exploration is encouraged and failure is not ridiculed then they learn that autonomy is prized. If not, they learn to feel shame and doubt their ability to survive in the world. As parents if we can balance out the endless "Nos" and "Don't touch!" with lots of positive messages and set up a safe environment for them to explore, then we encourage autonomy. Freud described this stage as being "the dry run for adolescence" as they explore the world away from us.

Stage 3 - Initiative versus Guilt

At this stage children start to assert themselves by planning activities, making up games, initiating play with others and asking lots of questions. If they are encouraged and not shamed they will learn that initiative and their ability to lead others and make decisions is prized. If they feel like they are a nuisance to others then they feel guilty.

Stage 4 - Industry versus Inferiority

This is when children are ready to be industrious - in my

opinion the countries around the world that do not start formal education until seven have got it right. Before this stage children are simply not ready to sit down and be industrious. They learn best through play, exploration and experimentation and to expect them to do otherwise is unhelpful. Sadly I think our obsession with hoop jumping and box ticking in education fails our children miserably. They need a culture of education that encourages a life long love of learning, that recognizes that participation in the arts and sport gives balance to our lives and whilst exams are, of course, important we are bigger than the certificates we collect. Whoops I have leapt onto my soapbox.... breathe and back to Stage 4.

This is a significant time because it is at this stage that the learning difficulties such as dyslexia, dyspraxia, ADHD etc are often first diagnosed and, if not carefully handled, these can get in the way of successful passage through Stage 4 leaving children feeling inferior. My daughter is dyslexic and I notice that despite overcoming the challenges that dyslexia poses and achieving great GCSE results, her confidence in her academic ability is still easily knocked. Stage 4 was tricky for her and unfortunately I didn't know all this stuff then so I wasn't much help!

Erikson's stages are like a stack of pound coins with each stage being represented by one coin. The flatter and straighter each coin is laid down the stronger the tower becomes. A tower with a foundation coin that sits on its edge will be wobbly and unstable. Nobody has a completely straight stack but if the tower is reasonably robust by the end of Stage 4 then we are well placed to manage the ups and downs of Stage 5 - Adolescence.

In a recent workshop one father asked me if Erikson's model is still relevant today and my answer was, yes. In therapy we use his model to establish where the developmental glitches are so that we can give clients an alternative experience. However, I think his Stage 5 age range is now wrong. The World Health Organisation defines an adolescent as a person between the ages of 10 and 19 but many parents I have spoken to think their 8 and 9 year olds are already displaying teenage behaviour and for others this behaviour continues well into their 20's.

And so to :-

Stage 5 - Adolescence - Identity versus Identity Diffusion
The developmental drive of this stage is to move from being a dependent child to being an independent adult with a clear sense of who we are and where we fit in the world. Finding our identity is about finding who we are as part of, but separate to our family. It is about developing our independence so that by the end of this stage we are ready to leave home and find our place in society as competent adults. Achieving this means changing the bond we have with our parents and trying out

different values, causes, looks, activities and friendship groups to find the ones that feel right.

It is important for us to understand the developmental drive through Stage 5 as it explains so much of what teenagers do. If they are to find their identity they must explore all aspects of themselves which explains the hideous music, weird and wonderful hair do's, random piercings and bizarre clothes. In the words of Logan Pearsall Smith, "Don't laugh at a youth for his affectations; he is only trying on one face after another to find a face of his own."

Frankly there is little incentive for most of our teenagers to leave the comfortable nest of Mum and Dad but the developmental drive for Identity means achieving autonomy. When they are tiny children they have a close bond with us. In order for them to form close attachments with others in later life, they need to change this bond and they do this via the peer group. So when the peer group seems all important and you feel like you are losing them to their friends, take heart: they are only doing what they need to do. I remember the sting I felt when my eldest first turned on me saying, "Oh Mum will you stop trying to be so down with the kids". It really hurt, I felt humiliated and upset and it took a few minutes to regain my equilibrium which was probably only possible because by this time I had done the training and recognized what was going on.

Some parents will attempt to protect themselves from the hurt their teenager's robust disrespect can cause by withdrawing, but this is a mistake. During adolescence I think our teenagers need us possibly more than at any other time as they are looking to us, the grown ups they know best, to see what it is to be an adult. The peer group is the place they will turn to for advice on immediate issues such as who to date or which music to listen to, but it is us that they look to for advice on the more important issues such as their moral code, values, education, job and career plans.

The peer group is the perfect place to try out relationships and social skills and it is where they will often get their emotional and social support from, but do not underestimate how important you still are to them. Take comfort in the knowledge that we are as important to them as we ever have been it just might not always feel like it.

Crossing the bridge from dependent child to independent adult is a huge challenge which requires change on every level and they need our love and support through this process. In the next chapter we are going to look at the changes that have to happen for them to achieve Autonomy and Identity because if we understand what is going on we are better placed to set them up for success and give their parrots useful information.

PS. Because the last three stages of Erikson's model are not relevant to this book I have decided not to explain them in detail. I apologise if you are wondering what Generativity vs Self Absorption is all about but you can find out online

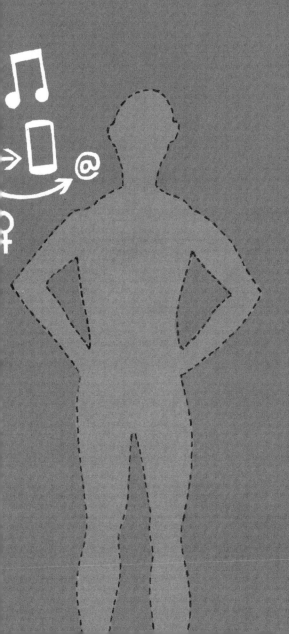

Chapter 3
ALL CHANGE

During adolescence teenagers change physically, emotionally and cognitively.

Physically I think we all have a pretty good idea about the changes happening to their bodies as they go through puberty and these don't generally cause too many problems unless they are happening at a different rate or in a different way to their peers.

Friends of mine have a son who is a fabulous sportsman and very tall for his age. When he arrived at his senior school he was regularly sent to the back of the lunch queue because the staff didn't believe he was a first year. Having to stand with pupils much older than him in those early days was frightening and he began to hate his size for singling him out. He said he felt like a giant and despite the fact that he had always had lots of female friends he stopped talking to the girls because he felt too big and clumsy. His sister's and mother's reassurances that most girls like tall boys fell on deaf ears, he just wanted to be the same height as the other boys in his year.

Thinking back to my teenage years I remember one of my most humiliating and toe curling moments happened when I was fifteen and a "friend" invited me and another friend to her Stone Age on the Rampage party. We arrived, with back combed hair, mud smeared over much of our bodies, black smudgy eyeliner, wooden clubs and some very small bits of faux fur only to find everyone else looking drop dead gorgeous in 1920s glitz! A cruel joke to play on anyone but particularly cruel to play on teenagers who just want to fit in and don't have the maturity to appreciate their finer qualities such as their great empathy or conversation skills!

Teenagers are constantly assessing themselves in terms of their physical appearance as was demonstrated by a study conducted by The Daily Mail which reported that the average woman looks in a mirror or reflective surface thirty eight times per day. The average man steals a peak on average eighteen times a day and the average teenager looks into a mirror or reflective surface a whopping sixty three times per day. Like it or not, how they look is of enormous importance to most of them and I say most because the subject for this book is the average teenager not the ones who go against the flow.

In general, the physical changes of adolescence are not problematic but be guided by your teen. I have met some who have the most horrendous acne but are totally unbothered by it and others who have a couple of spots but the end of their world is nigh. If your teenager is bothered then take them seriously, remember your own insecurities at that age; show empathy and if there is something you can do to help then do it. For example, your GP has a positive battery of ammunition to combat spots.

"At fourteen you don't need sickness or death for tragedy"
Jessamyn West

When it comes to their feelings teenagers are all over the place and the emotional roller coaster that is adolescence can feel frightening and overwhelming for them.

Too numerous are the times I have sat with teenagers who are utterly bewildered by the speed at which their feelings can change from high to low and back again. A friend of mine who is going through the menopause said "I just don't know what is going on, I keep bursting into tears" and I thought, "if you haven't worked it out after years of hormonal changes no wonder these kids get hijacked!"

Sometimes just helping them to understand that the hormones required to make the physical changes to their bodies are partly to blame for their changes in mood can come as an enormous relief to them. Pre-Menstrual Syndrome (PMS) is an acknowledged cause of irritability and mild depression but why should teenage girls know this? We may not be able to stop the symptoms but we can at least take away the fear.

Likewise, as their bodies are changing so is their world as they are expected to take on more and more responsibility. Suddenly finding that you are expected to be able to motivate and organize yourself, to run your own diary and make your own travel and social arrangements can be rather a shock. They might be struggling with their relationships with friends as they try to find where they fit. They are likely to experience increased pressure at school as important external exams loom. Add to this mix their first exposure to sex, drugs, parties and alcohol and suddenly there is a lot for them to deal with.

A part of growing up is developing the skills to deal with this pressure but it takes time and in the interim they need our love and understanding. They need us to be on hand to listen which will usually be at the most inconvenient time for you.

It always seems to be last thing at night just when I am feeling totally poleaxed and ready to drop that they need a DMC (Deep and Meaningful Conversation to you and me).

As parents we know how horrible it can be to feel stuck in painful feelings. We love them and we don't want them to feel bad so we employ a raft of techniques to try to make them feel better.

Imagine this scenario. Your teenager discovers that a friend is having a party and they haven't been invited. You can see they are upset and want to help.

"Never mind, come on let's go and watch a film" - Distracting

"You're fine - just forget about it" - Denying

"Well perhaps if you hadn't had a go at her on Tuesday she would have invited you" - Criticising

"It's only one party, there'll be others" - Minimising

"Woe is me, the end of the world is nigh - you'll probably never be invited to another party again!" - Sarcasm

Does one sound like something you might say?

The trouble with all these responses is that they leave your teen with a double problem. "I feel the way I feel and now you're saying I'm not allowed to feel like that, aargh!"

No feeling, good or bad, lasts forever and the fastest way out of any feeling is straight through the middle of it. In other words if you allow your teen to experience the disappointment and hurt they will be able to move on from it more quickly and easily. We can achieve this by showing that we are trying to understand how they might be feeling, saying something like, "It can be really horrible to discover you have been left out of something, I guess you might be feeling really upset."

We don't have magic wands so we can't fix all their problems and we would do them a massive disservice if we did. Dealing with disappointment is a tough but important lesson to learn. We show them that we care when we try to see things from their perspective; acknowledge their feelings and ask them what they need. Beware of giving advice when emotions are running high as it is rarely well received. I fell into this particularl trap recently and was firmly put back in my place with "Mum, shut up, I don't want you to do anything I just want you to listen!"

Many teenagers think they are the only ones going through

the emotional mill. When I ask the teenagers that I see in therapy what they want from counselling it is amazing how many "just want to check that I am normal". Even exploring the idea of "normal" can be really helpful. It is normal to feel unsure about who you are and where you are heading; it is normal to swing between wanting to leave home and finding the whole idea frightening; it is normal to feel unsure about where you fit in friendship groups; it is normal to have periods of low mood during adolescence.

However, a word of caution here, there is a world of difference between occasional low mood and depression which can be a serious mental illness requiring treatment. The following list can all be signs of depression and if you are unsure whether or not you should be seeking help for your teenager, consider how long the symptoms have been present, how severe they are and how different they seem to their normal selves.

Loss of appetite, sadness, restlessness, irritation, anger, aggression, tearfulness, feelings that life is meaningless, withdrawal from family and friends, fatigue, lack of energy, agitation, loss of interest or enthusiasm in previously enjoyed activities, change in sleeping habits, change in eating habits, significant weight gain or loss, difficulty in concentrating or organizing themselves, change in performance at school, frequent complaints of physical pain.

Depression is not going to be a problem for most teenagers but it is more difficult to diagnose than it is in adults because it can be hard to distinguish from normal adolescent behaviour. If we know our teenagers well and are armed with the facts, then we are better placed to help them. If you are worried please don't bury your head in the sand because the success rates for treating teenage depression are good but too many are left to fend for themselves and sometimes this may prove to be too much.

In conclusion, mood swings are normal but are not much fun for those experiencing them or for their nearest and dearest. When I get my head bitten off for the tenth time in a day I console myself with the thought that they don't snap at their friends, their friends parents or their teachers. As parents we are likely to bear the brunt of their mood swings for two reasons. Firstly because they are trying to change their bond with us and secondly, because they know we love them we give them a safe place to let off steam - it's a compliment really!

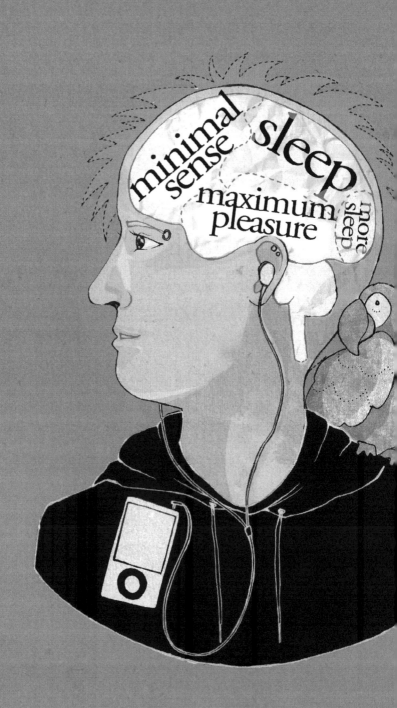

Chapter 4
THE TEEN BRAIN EXPLAINED

Listen up because you're wired all wrong!

As THE BODIES AND EMOTIONS OF TEENAGERS CHANGE, SO DO THEIR brains. In fact the teenage brain is a fascinating place to explore and understanding what is going on can really help us to view them in a positive light and improve our parrot programming.

Scientists once thought that the brain was fully formed by the end of childhood but thanks to the invention of functional magnetic resonance imaging machines (fMRI) we now know this to be far from the truth. Neuroscientists have made some astonishing discoveries about the changing structure of the teenage brain and if you are interested in the detailed technical explanations then I recommend a book called "The Primal Teen" by Barbara Strauch. If you prefer the layman's version then read on.

In early adolescence there is a massive increase in the number of neurones (brain cells) in the pre-frontal cortex. This growth peaks by eleven for girls and twelve for boys. The pre-frontal cortex is the area of the brain that weighs up outcome, reads other people, controls logic and makes judgement decisions.

You would assume that having a load more brain cells in this area would be a good thing but unfortunately it is not so simple. There are too many neurones for them to operate effectively, they need pruning and the connections between them need strengthening because it is the quality of the connections that matter not the number of neurones. Imagine a rose bush that isn't pruned. The stems become long and whippy with very few roses - if you prune it well it may look smaller but the branches become stronger and the number of roses increases. Our brains are similar. As the neurones are pruned and we build strong pathways by repeatedly using them (this is the use it or lose it bit) our pre-frontal cortex becomes more and more effective.

The pruning of the neurones carries on until sixteen for girls and seventeen for boys and whilst it is happening their pre-frontal cortex is not at its most effective. In other words it should come as no surprise that they make poor choices from time to time.

This summer my girls went to the USA to stay with their

American cousins for two weeks and, wanting their holiday to start well, I sent them off to buy presents. Several hours later they reappeared with a promising array of shopping bags and the kitchen table was soon covered in lovely things that they had bought for themselves and one yellow, plastic Marmite toast cutter for their cousins. Whilst I could have cheerfully murdered them I did have to laugh - narcissism, thinking things through - why was I surprised?

When you send them off to revise and then discover that they have spent the time on Facebook, don't be shocked - teens are much more in the moment than we are and they are simply not wired to have thought through the long term consequences.

TOP TIP *To help them stay on track with revision - suggest that they divide the topic up into small sections so that they don't overwhelm themselves before they start. Then set an alarm for twenty minutes and explain that they can only work for that amount of time. Once the time is up suggest that they take a small break and then go back for another twenty minutes. None of us can concentrate fully for much more than twenty minutes so it is more productive to do three sessions of twenty than try to sit down and study for an hour.*

The part of the teenage brain that is operating very sensitively is the limbic system. It is the brain's pleasure, reward and impulsivity zone and it is sensitively tuned during adolescence which means that teenagers need a much higher level of stimulus than a child or an adult to achieve the same buzz which perhaps explains why they do some crazy things.

I was chatting to one school head recently who was despairing of his Year 10 boys (14ish) several of whom were currently off sport with broken ankles or legs. When I asked how they had hurt themselves he said, "the latest craze is jumping off the harbour wall which is absolutely fine when the tide is in but not so fine when there are only six inches of water!" We laughed, but it is interesting because really they were only doing what they are designed to do at this stage, namely, to fit in with the peer group; to find weighing up outcome difficult; to take risks; seek pleasure and to test personal boundaries.

With their underdeveloped pre frontal cortex and overly tuned limbic system, teenagers are unhelpfully wired : maximum thrill seeking and minimum sense. So what is the advantage of this crazy brain set up? Why are they wired this way?

A fledgling bird prepares to leave its nest by flapping its wings, then it moves onto the edge of the nest to gain more space to flap and hop about. Then it might experiment with flying by flapping its way to the next door branch until eventually it is ready to take the death defying swoop out into the big, blue yonder. If you think about it, by the end of adolescence teenagers need to be ready to leave home and go it alone in the adult world : experimentation helps them to be ready for the next step.

Another explanation could be evolutionary. Throughout history teenage boys have been expected to go out and hunt or fight wars. Perhaps if they had had the ability to weigh up outcome and assess their vulnerability they would have been less inclined to sally forth. Their poor risk assessment skills allow them to feel invulnerable, even omnipotent, after all, taking a risk isn't a problem if you genuinely believe that you won't experience bad consequences : it won't happen to me.

We have covered the brain science bit but why is it important? Well, if we understand that their brain is rather unhelpfully wired at this stage then we can train their parrot to compensate and we will explore this in later chapters. Before we move on from cognitive development there are a couple of other tips that as parents of teenagers you might find handy.

As I mentioned at the beginning of this chapter, the prefrontal cortex is also responsible for reading other people. The fact that it is not firing on all cylinders during adolescence might be enough of a reason for teenagers to find reading facial expressions difficult, However, through the use of fMRI scanning, scientists have found an even more interesting explanation. Adults use their pre-frontal cortex to read other people whereas teenagers use their limbic system which is the instinctive rather than the thinking part of the brain. I decided to do my own, admittedly somewhat unscientific experiment to see how easy or difficult they find it to read facial expressions.

I made a chart of six different facial expressions and asked teenagers to identify what emotion each face expressed. I have now done this with approximately two hundred and sixty 13 - 15 year olds and to date only three have read all six expressions correctly. When I tried the same experiment with staff and adult friends their hit rate was miles higher with over half getting 100%. Interestingly the one expression that foxed most of the teenagers was "worried". Invariably they read it as angry : for us parents that has huge implications.

Imagine going into your teenager's bedroom (always a soul destroying experience in my younger daughter's pig sty) and they are lying on their bed in semi darkness listening to music. On the desk you notice a half completed essay. With your best concerned face in place you ask if they are confident that they are going to get it finished on time. I can write about this with no trouble because it happened very recently, "Why don't you trust me? I know when it has to be in and I'm on it, OK. Just leave me alone!" was my daughter's response. The vehemence of her reply stunned me and it took me a couple of minutes to gather myself together sufficiently to ask her why she had flown at me. I thought I had been showing mild concern but she said she thought I was angry with her which gave a great deal more meaning to her defensive attack.

TOP TIP *If you feel that you and your teenager have crossed wires it might well be that they have misread you. Check it out with them because it is amazing how often they get it wrong.*

Sleep

... and finally on the brain. When your teenager complains that he can't get to sleep even though you are sure he is tired and it is late, he may well be telling the truth. Equally, early mornings are something that most teens could miss for a decade if it weren't for the inconvenience of school. This change in sleep patterns during adolescence is attributable to another change in their brain.

The Pineal Gland is a part of the endocrine system and it produces several important hormones including Melatonin. Melatonin influences sexual development and regulates the sleep-wake cycle. During adolescence the Pineal Gland produces Melatonin at different times which affects the body's internal clock or circadian rhythms. In the run up to adolescence the circadian rhythms send children towards the land of nod at about 8pm but, the change in the release of Melatonin during adolescence, means that many teenagers will struggle to get to sleep by 11pm or even much later.

Teenagers need an average of nine hours sleep per night even if they dropped off at 11pm on the dot and woke for school at 7am they would be missing out on one hour per night. Over the course of the week they would be sleep deprived by a minimum of five hours and sleep deprivation is not good for us. It causes irritability, loss of concentration and mood swings - sound familiar? We cannot change the time they need to get to school, although some schools are trialling a later start time, but we can let them catch up on sleep at the weekend and here are some tips to help them maximise the amount of sleep they get.

1. The light from back lit computer and tablet screens has the same effect as drinking a double expresso? Ideally get them to put their screens away 45 minutes before they need to go to sleep. If they can't be persuaded that this is a good plan at least get them to turn the brightness on the screen right down.

2. Having a regular routine helps our body to recognise when it should be settling down for sleep.

3. Warm baths or showers and milky drinks help to make us sleepy.

4. If all else fails, feed them turkey which contains Tryptophan - an essential amino acid that aids sleep. Perhaps this also explains why we fall asleep after Christmas dinner.

TOP TIP *If you are struggling to get your teenagers out of bed in the morning here is a handy hint. Walking into their room and flinging their curtains open is an inefficient way to wake a teenager. This is because the Pineal Gland, which in adults and children reacts to morning light, doesn't work in the same way in teenagers. I am always amazed at how they can sleep until noon in a room with no curtains but it can be scientifically explained.*

The best way to wake a teenager is to make enough noise (be kind) until you see something move, a twitch of a toe is enough, then go away and leave them for ten minutes. When you go back in, open the curtains, turn on the music and make sure they are awake. This is THE TEN MINUTE RULE and it is golden because ten minutes represents the amount of time it takes for us to shift from a deep sleep cycle to a lighter one. Once in the lighter cycle they should find it much easier to get going.

You now have the lowdown on how your teenager is wired and programmed to operate during adolescence. They need to find their identity as part of, but separate to, their family. This drive is both strong and necessary and we need to work with it unless we want to spend the best part of a decade feeling thoroughly frustrated. They find their identity through experimentation and their brain set up means that they are likely to take greater risks than we would. Hold all of this in your thoughts and let's start programming their parrots.

Chapter 5
PARROTS ON-LINE

Safety check – excellent!

PRIVACY SETTINGS

☐ PRIVATE
☐ NOT PRIVATE

I HAVE BEEN FORTUNATE IN HAVING A WONDERFUL COLLEAGUE, Ellen Ferguson of The Family Friendly Net to help me with this chapter. Ellen is an internet safety advisor and I like her approach because, like me, she believes that if parents and schools can set teenagers up to be successful online then they can get the best out of the internet. They become critical consumers of online content and know how to keep themselves safe. So much more positive and productive than freaking them out with horror stories about the dark side of the cyber world.

At the beginning of every Let's Talk Teens Workshop I ask parents what they want to get out of the session and someone will always ask for tips on how to keep them safe on line. Unlike us our teenagers were born into a digital world, for them the online world is just an extension of their offline world. Most of my friends are reasonably at home on-line but they are streets behind their offspring when it comes to adopting and understanding new technology.

Do you remember the story about the Mosquito, a device that emitted a pulsed high frequency tone only audible to young people and which was used to deter groups of teenagers from loitering in public places such as shopping centres? It caused a great deal of controversy on the basis of human rights but the teens got the last laugh as they turned it into a ring tone for their phones meaning they could keep them on during lessons. I have been unable to establish whether or not this last snippet is an urban myth, but either way I think it makes the point rather well. Unless you are uber computer savvy your teenagers will always be one step ahead of you in the digital world.

So what messages do their parrots need to give them so that they can enjoy all the wonderful things that the internet and social media offers them whilst keeping themselves safe online? This section of parrot programming requires you to have a reasonable grip on the basics of internet safety and be courageous enough to have the right conversations and ask the right questions.

Most parents are pretty good at monitoring the computer use of younger children and have parental controls in place to prevent them from accessing adult or unsuitable content.

TOP TIP *If you are struggling to keep up at this level there are routers on the market that will allow you to set each member of your family up with different levels of access so that your 11 year old can't access social media sites but your 14 year old can. These routers can also put time limiters on to each person's use.*

However as they enter teendom it becomes increasingly difficult to monitor their use of the internet as they are less inclined to show us what they are doing or share their passwords and access codes. This is part of their quest for independence. Another complicating factor is that the internet is accessible on so many different devices from the television to the gaming console and even if you can deny them access to your wifi service they are probably able to tap into another one.

Some parents remove all electronic devices from their teens as they go upstairs to bed. I am of the belief that this is the sticking plaster approach - removing the immediate problem does not teach them how to use technology appropriately. If, after training, your teenager is unable to limit their usage or use the technology responsibly then, by all means, cut them off. This is never going to be popular but most teens expect to get their mobile phones or laptops removed at some point.

A conversation that I think helps and which gives us licence to take control back if they are unable to act responsibly, might go something like this:

"*My job as your parent is to keep you safe. Your job is to go for independence. Believe it or not I really want you to get there because, although I love you to pieces, I am sure neither of us really want you to be living at home when you are forty. I imagine it as being a little bit like having you on a long piece of elastic. I want you to take the elastic and pull away and when the day comes that you are good to go we will cut the elastic and you will be free. In the meantime however, if I think you are not ready or able to keep yourself safe, I reserve the right to tweak the elastic and hoick you back in line until you have proved you are ready to take back control and move forward responsibly. I know this may sound really annoying but we need to work together.*"

Acknowledging how they might feel shows that you are trying to see things from their perspective which reduces resistance.

Teens use the internet in a very different way to us so it is important to chat to them about what they are doing online. I regularly recruit my teens to teach me how to use different programmes and apps because I figure that then I have at least a vague understanding of what they are up to. Some of the questions you need to be asking are:

Do you understand privacy settings and are you using them?

Do you know that it is important to check privacy settings regularly because even the biggest service providers can have occasional breaches of security?

Do you know how to block messages from unwelcome contacts?

Do you know how to find safety advice online if you need it?

Do you know not to give out any personal information?

If you made a friend online who you then wanted to meet in person how do you think you could do it safely?

Do you know how to untag photos or that it is ok to ask others to untag photos?

Which services would you be happy to use webcam for?

We need to talk to them about what they are sharing on line because their Digital Footprint (everything about them that is on the internet) is going to be something that all future colleges, universities and employers will look at. I read a wonderful story about a teacher who was trying to get the message about digital footprints across to his pupils. He invited one up on stage, gave him a huge piece of paper and a bottle of tomato ketchup and asked him to draw a picture of himself. Once the portrait was complete the head showed it to the rest of the school and then turned to the boy and asked him to put the ketchup back in the bottle. The penny dropped. It is boring but digital footprints really do matter so get your teen to search for themselves on-line regularly to see what comes up. I have even met headmasters who check out a family's digital footprint before deciding whether or not to offer a child a place.

Some parents will ask what the point is in discussing the long term importance of their digital footprint if teenagers live in the moment and can't think that far ahead. Well the point is this: if you don't have these conversations with them then you can't be sure that they know this stuff. I am not saying that simply having a conversation will definitely stop them doing ridiculous things, but with awareness comes choice. If their parrot is well informed when that moment of choice arises perhaps they will make the right one rather than the wrong one.

And so the parrot programming goes on...

You need to consider how someone might feel before you post a photo of them on-line.

Would you be happy to say that to their face?

Would you be happy to walk down the high street with that on the front of your T-shirt because if not do you think it is appropriate to put it online?

How are you going to know where that piece of information ends up?

Who are you going to turn to if you think an adult is posing as a teenager to talk to you?

What can you do and who can you tell if you are bullied online?

TOP TIP *Interestingly, many parents seem anxious about their teenagers' use of the big social networking sites such as Facebook, Instagram, YouTube and Twitter but the bigger sites tend to be safer as they invest huge amounts of energy, time and money into ensuring their users' safety. They have terms and conditions that stipulate what* *material can and cannot be posted and, if you come across content that contravenes these terms and you contact them, they will remove it. For parents there is a page on most of the big sites explaining what their site does and how you can help your kids to use it safely.*

Most of the big social networking sites also have a minimum joining age. Many parents I meet have allowed their children to lie about their age to set up an account but what they fail to appreciate is that the big sites show adverts that are age appropriate so your kids might find themselves exposed to content that is aimed at older teens.

I was working with a group of Year 8 pupils recently who had come across an app where you could post a photo of yourself and ask others to give it a tagline. It sounded like fun but caused huge upset when some of the tags were unpleasant. There was no support system that you could contact to report the abuse and the app now seems to have disappeared leaving behind a very sour taste.

Young people need to know that there is a dark side to the internet and that there are people out there who will use it as a means to find their targets for abuse but that this happens to a minority of people. We need to get the message across LOUD

AND CLEAR that they must NEVER, under any circumstance, agree to meet someone in person whom they have only met online unless they set up the meeting responsibly, ie they take an adult with them. We don't want to frighten them but they need to know how to stay safe.

Most adults I meet scoff at the number of friends their teenagers tell them they have online. What we need to remember is that "friends" means something very different to them - they are friends of friends, people they have met gaming or in chat rooms. They just want to fit in and having loads of "friends" on Facebook can make you feel less alone. When I joined Twitter I shocked myself by how excited I got every time I acquired a new follower! This stuff can boost our confidence but it does come with a flip side because being connected 24/7 can be extremely stressful. When we weren't invited to a party we probably didn't even know about it until a few days after the event. Today they know they have been excluded as the party is going on and seeing your friends having fun without you on a social media site can be really upsetting.

I mentioned Cyberbullying but didn't give you any tips on what to do if it happens. Again there are great websites to help you and your children but here is the quick heads up:-

1. Offer reassurance and confirm that they are being bullied

2. Help them to keep the evidence

3. Report the incident to the provider of the medium on which the bullying is taking place eg mobile phone or website as they can remove content and block the perpetrator.

4.If appropriate, report the incident to the police. Although bullying isn't a criminal offence there are five criminal and civil laws that can apply such as The Protection from Harassment Act 1997.

5.If they find content about themselves that they are uncomfortable with the quickest way to lose it is to bury it by being very busy online. Set up a blog and write posts often, contribute to online discussions and get tweeting because this will all make it harder for other users to find the negative content.

A word on downloading. Many teens use the internet to download films, music and games software and, because teenagers are usually strapped for cash it can be tempting to download them for free. Generally free content of this nature is of a lower quality than the paid stuff and users run the risk of downloading a load of net nasties such as viruses, spyware and adware along with their chosen items. The Digital Economy

Act of 2010 has yet to be implemented but, it contains a plan to have a three strike approach to copyright infringement which could mean that parents receive a letter explaining that someone in their house has been downloading copyrighted material illegally. This could lead to a fine, a slowed service or a court summons. In the Useful Resources section you will find a website to help you and your family to download legally and avoid any of these possible penalties.

And finally. There is a lot of research to show that teenagers are less likely to turn to their parents if they encounter a problem online than offline and this is probably because they are scared we might stop them using it. Make it clear to your teen that you are there for them if something bad happens and that you won't cut them off but will work with them to sort the problem out. There are a number of great websites with information for parents, teenagers and children on how to stay safe on line and you will find them in the Useful Resources section. There is a lot in this chapter and it will need to be drip fed to them over time however, if you cover all of this with your teens they will have internet savvy parrots who just might make them stop and think before they click OPEN or SEND.

EVERY TEENAGER NEEDS A PARROT

THE IDEA OF OUR CHILDREN BECOMING SEXUAL BEINGS IS OFTEN AN uncomfortable one for parents. Somehow, once they have crossed this particular bridge we are forced to face the fact that our babies are now very definitely becoming adults and it won't be long before they are flying the nest.

Unfortunately, sex and relationships are topics that many parents struggle to discuss with their teenagers and yet it is so important. If we don't, they will seek knowledge elsewhere and today their most likely port of call is the internet. There are lots of good, factual sites that they could access for information but the danger is that if they are looking for sex related topics they are only a few clicks away from some pretty hardcore pornography. According to the Techcrunch website, 12% of all sites online and 25% of all searches are porn related and the average age at which most children will first access it is eleven. Remember that this is the AVERAGE age which means that some children must be looking at porn at much younger ages. Many parents don't believe that their teenagers will come across pornography but the statistics say otherwise.

We have established that teenagers are designed to push boundaries and seek reward : cyber erotica can provide an easy way to achieve both. However, because of the brain rewiring that is going on at this stage, the sexual proclivities that they pick up in early adolescence can be difficult to change as they get older. We don't want our teens to be unable to achieve orgasm without watching or acting out violent or degrading scenes from pornography sites.

Unlike the porn magazines that our generation might have looked at, the internet provides moving images which form much more vivid and lasting memories that can be difficult to wipe from our minds. I recently heard about a twelve year old boy who had gone to his friend's 13th birthday party. After supper the parents disappeared and the birthday boy accessed a porn film on the computer and masturbated in front of his friends. Since the party the boy was having trouble sleeping, was tearful and reliving scenes from the film. This child was traumatized and needed help, which he got, but the whole sorry situation raised bigger issues because the parents holding the party could have been sued under the tort of negligence for failing to control their child and social services would have been involved.

We all know that kids sometimes end up on inappropriate sites by mistake. I heard of one fifteen year old boy who, when aged nine, mistakenly typed "orgasm" instead of "organism" into a search engine whilst doing research for a biology project. The top of the first page was ok with scientific definitions but as he scrolled down there were adverts for free porn videos and, being an inquisitive little chap, he explored. Six years later he was a frequent user of hardcore porn sites who couldn't have a real life relationship because in his words 'it wasn't exciting enough'. Repeatedly viewing graphic, violent and abusive sex had left him desensitized and with a profoundly flawed view of sexual intimacy.

The porn industry is huge and whilst not as profitable as it was in the early days of the internet, it is still extremely lucrative. These films are made by men for men and rarely show anything that treats women with respect or shows intimate love making. If our kids get the idea that anal sex, gagging and spitting represent intimacy then I think they are on a sad and emotionally lonely road. It is important for us to get the message across that sex without any form of emotional attachment is the opposite of intimacy and for most of us, one without the other makes for a pretty barren experience.

The thing about sex is that it embraces the widest possible range of human tastes and a part of teenagers finding their identity means discovering where their tastes lie. Experimentation is ok providing both parties are happy with what is going on; that the timing is right for both of them and that there is no coercion.

In terms of parrot programming there are lots of messages that are important:

1. Deciding when to lose your virginity is one of the big decisions of adolescence and it is ok to wait until you feel ready. It is not a race and the average age for losing your virginity in the UK in 2013 is 16 (a lot later than most of the teenagers I work with think). This does not mean that 16 is the target age it is the AVERAGE age (not to mention the first time it is legal) i.e. lots of teenagers wait considerably longer. In a BBC survey of sexually active 12 to 17 year olds, 63% said they wished they had waited longer. If your teenager knows this, it might give them the confidence to wait until they feel that the time is right for them.

2. Many teens consider oral sex to be "safe" but the truth is that it is the most common way of passing on a sexually transmitted infection (STI).

3. Teenagers need to know that it is important for them to use a condom to stop them catching or transmitting STI's as well as to prevent unwanted pregnancy. If we can get the message across that partners who refuse

to wear a condom are showing gross disrespect then perhaps they will chose to walk away rather than put themselves at risk.

TOP TIP *Get them thinking about what they might say if faced with any of the following reasons for not using a condom:-*

a. It's uncomfortable

b. I lose the mood when I stop to put one on

c. Don't you trust me?

d. I can't enjoy sex if I use one

If they have thought this stuff through in advance they are much more likely to be able to refuse unprotected sex.

4. Once teenagers become sexually active we need to encourage them to go for regular checkups because some STI's such as Chlamydia have no immediate symptoms but can cause long term problems such as infertility.

5. Both boys and girls need to know that forcing anyone to perform sexual acts of any kind is called sexual assault or rape and it is a crime.

6. They need accurate information about sex but it is just as important to talk about relationships, feelings, attitudes and values.

What do you think a healthy relationship might look like?

What is intimacy? How might couples show that they love one another?

Do you think it is ok if your partner stops you seeing your friends?

Is violence in a relationship ever ok?

What could you do if you felt unsafe in a relationship?

How important is your reputation to you?

What do you think could spoil your reputation?

As you can see, parrot programming relies on open and honest communication. It can be hard to bring up the topic of sex but there is always plenty about it on the TV, in the papers and even in music lyrics. Use these to start a conversation. If you are talking about risks then present them objectively and accurately - no scaremongering please. Don't wait for the "right moment" as it is unlikely to come along just use any opportunities that present themselves.

I had a really interesting conversation about sexting with my girls after reading about the tragic story of a young girl throwing herself off a balcony after her ex-boyfriend refused to delete a revealing photo of her from his phone. Sexting is the practice of texting sexually explicit messages, photos or videos of yourself or someone else to another person and it is popular practice amongst today's teenagers. Because teens are poor at considering long term outcome we need to talk to them about the possible consequences.

If you split up who is going to have possession of those photos and what might they do with them?

How would you feel if his/her phone was accessed by someone else or stolen and the photos ended up in the wrong hands? Your reputation is your responsibility.

Do you think there are better ways to show someone that you love them than sexting?

Did you know that it is illegal to have indecent images or videos of under 18's in your possession?

Did you know that it is illegal to distribute or share indecent images or video of under 18's?

In April 2013 three teenagers in Virginia USA, who had passed around "sexts" of an underage friend were prosecuted for distributing child pornography. Similar cases have been brought in Australia and I don't suppose it will be too long before it happens in the UK as stricter anti-child pornography laws are introduced.

In conclusion, talking to your teenagers about relationships and sex is vital and ideally they need to hear from both their mums and dads so that they get a rounded perspsective on relationships, expectations and appropriate behaviour. Talking helps teenagers to formulate their values and fills their parrot with information that can be used to keep them safe; talking helps to give them the confidence to explore at the time and speed that feels right for them; talking helps them to recognise the difference between a healthy and an unhealthy relationship; talking helps them to learn to listen to the needs of their partner and to ask for their own needs to be met. I know it is hard but I am sure you can do it and if all else fails I guess you could give them this to read.

Chapter 7
PARROTS ON ALCOHOL

FOR MOST PARENTS DRUGS ARE A HIGHLY EMOTIVE SUBJECT. We know that teenagers are designed to experiment but we have all heard the horror stories and this is one area in which we would really rather they didn't dabble. When we talk about drugs we tend to think of marijuana, cocaine, ecstasy etc but it is also important to include alcohol and tobacco for three reasons. Firstly because they are likely to be the first drugs that your children encounter; secondly because they are the most accessible drugs and thirdly because alcohol is the drug that is likely to cause your teenagers the most problems.

So let's start with alcohol and cigarettes.

As I mentioned in Chapter 2, teenagers are looking to us to see what it is to be an adult in this world and the modelling that we provide for them has a huge impact on their behavior. In a 2011 survey commissioned by The Joseph Rowntree Foundation, researchers found that teenagers who saw their parents drinking or drunk were far more likely to drink regularly and to excess.

We need to think about our attitude towards alcohol and the messages that we are sending to our teens because we exert a great deal more influence than we perhaps imagine. Culturally, alcohol has become the acceptable drug of choice it is, therefore, easy to get the messages wrong. However, as I discovered recently, this can have surprising results: It was a Friday night and I said to my husband, "I'm exhausted, I need a glass of wine". As quick as a flash from the other end of the kitchen came a quiet voice, "Mum I think you are confusing your needs and your wants." Mmmm.... out of the mouths of babes! Is it not both satisfying and unnerving when roles are reversed?

I have met very few parents who have given their teenagers the message that alcohol abstinence is a perfectly valid choice. Most parents want to know when and how to introduce it safely. The research suggests that the younger we introduce it to children the greater the likelihood that they will drink as teenagers and drink to excess. Advice from the NHS is that children should not drink before fifteen because those who do drink regularly before this age are five times more likely to be heavy drinkers as adults. Teenagers who drink to excess are seven times more likely to be involved in a car accident and eleven times more likely to be hurt in an alcohol related accident than their non-drinking peers. As for the effect alcohol has on their developing brains, well it is a difficult area of research but scientists have already made a couple of very interesting discoveries.

Firstly that alcohol does not make adolescents as sleepy as it makes adults. This should be a comforting thought but it really isn't because it means that instead of nodding off when they have had too much to drink they may be emboldened to try something more daring when their pre-frontal cortex is even less efficient than it normally is.

Secondly, because their brains are undergoing such a huge restructuring programme during adolescence they are particularly sensitive to alcohol and even very small amounts can have a marked effect on their long term learning ability.

It never ceases to amaze me how few parents have talked to their teenagers about drink by the time they hit thirteen. New research out from the charity Drinkaware suggests that thirteen is the average age for a teenager to have their first alcoholic drink (and again we are talking averages so some are experimenting earlier).

It is important to give teenagers the message that they don't have to drink but I have seen too many run into difficulties too young to believe that this is enough. We need to educate them about alcohol so that they can take responsibility for their drinking and, once again, this means being proactive rather than reactive in programming their parrots.

When I talk to young teenagers about alcohol I show them a 330ml (4% proof) bottle of lager, a small glass ie 125ml wine, a 275ml (standard size WKD) alcopop and a 30ml (40% proof) shot of vodka and I ask them which one has the most alcohol in it. Invariably they will say the vodka though the truth is that they all have about 1.4 units.

I then ask them :

> **"What is a unit of alcohol?"** A unit of alcohol is a measure of the volume of pure alcohol in an alcoholic drink.
>
> **"Which drink has the largest volume?"** Lager
>
> **"Which drink will fill you up the quickest?"** Lager
>
> **"If there are 330ml in the bottle of lager and 30ml in the shot of vodka how many shots would you have to down to drink the same volume of liquid?"** Eleven
>
> **"I am absolutely not encouraging you to drink but, if you**

choose to, then at least think about what you are going to drink because... you will run out of space before you fall flat on your face with the lager, the wine or the alcopop but you will fall flat on your face long before you run out of space if you go for the shots."

"If you choose to drink then try and drink a non-alcoholic drink after every alcoholic one."

"If you drink remember that if things that don't normally move start moving it is time to stop!"

I think it is fair to say that, over recent years, there has been a seismic shift in the way that some teenagers use alcohol. As teenagers, most of us drank to feel more confident whereas now many teenagers drink to get drunk and they do it in spectacular fashion. As parents we need to get them thinking through the implications of drinking to excess:-

What do you think could happen if you drink too much?

How might you feel the day after if you have vomited all over someone's house?

How might you feel the day after if you can't remember what you said or did?

How are you going to keep yourself safe?

How are you going to protect your reputation?

If you are really drunk, how easy do you think it will be to say no if someone asks you to do something you aren't sure about?"

If one of your friends is really drunk what will you do to help them to stay safe?

This may all seem very obvious to you and I but these are not questions your average thirteen year old will have thought about.

There is a bit more about alcohol in the Parrots on Parties chapter so let's move on to smoking.

Statistically the number of teenagers who smoke has fallen year on year since 2000 to an all time low of 11% in 2011. As with alcohol, if you smoke then they are more likely to. In fact three times more likely to. Equally, if their siblings or peers smoke and if cigarettes are easy to get hold of, then they are more likely to smoke. Attitudes towards smoking have changed dramatically in recent years. In 1999 50% of children thought it was acceptable to try smoking compared to 35% today which is all great news and means we are heading in the right direction.

I recognize that smoking is a button pushing subject for many parents and I don't suppose any of us want our teenagers to smoke. For me perhaps the most compelling reason to push for abstinence is that if they don't smoke cigarettes they are much less likely to smoke cannabis. The line I have taken has been, "Whether or not you smoke is up to you. I don't want you to because it is not only bad for your health but extremely difficult to give up. I am sure you will be offered a cigarette at some stage and then you are going to have to make your own mind up so think it through. Is this something you want in your life and if the answer is no, how could you refuse?"

Other parents adopt other methods. One father who caught his son smoking made him sit down and chain smoke the rest of the packet - he was sick but history doesn't relate whether or not it was effective as a long term deterrent. Another had a party for her seventeen year old daughter and decided to provide cigarettes. She knew they all smoked and she felt it was more dangerous to risk them wandering off site to replenish their stocks, which would involve crossing several busy roads when they had had a few drinks, than to have a supply on standby.

And finally, a friend who discovered her son was smoking cut his allowance on the basis that if he had money for cigarettes she was obviously giving him too much.

Whatever your approach, remember that very few teenagers make an active decision to become smokers, they make a choice in a moment to try a cigarette. If we arm them with the facts about smoking and then hand over responsibility, we devalue smoking as a boundary pusher. We give them a sense of choice, control and ownership which may make the forbidden fruit look less tasty

THERE ARE MANY EXCELLENT WEBSITES THAT YOU CAN ACCESS IF YOU want to be well informed about drugs and I have listed some in the Really Useful Section. For the purpose of this book I have attempted to give you enough information to be able to talk to your teenagers and programme their parrots but it is a vast topic and any extra research you choose to undertake can only be beneficial.

Whether or not your teen decides to experiment with drugs will depend on a number of factors the most important being the messages you give them and the attitude and influence of their peer group. Peer pressure can make it incredibly difficult for some teenagers to "just say no" so discuss with them what they could say instead. Here are ideas that some of the teenagers I work with have come up with:

I can't I'm on antibiotics

Sorry I have got a big match/training session tomorrow

I can't because they do random drug testing at school/ in my club.

Drugs are not my thing, I would rather drink

I'm allergic

The important thing here is that these are the teenagers' ideas not mine and because they are theirs they are much more likely to be able to use them should they be faced with the choice. Reassuringly many teens seem very confident that they will be able to give a straight no but it is still important to have the discussion because it is one conversation that really could save their lives.

I couldn't possibly detail all the drugs that are available so I have limited myself to looking at the ones that are currently most commonly available to teenagers. If you are interested in others have a look at www.talktofrank.com which has an entire A-Z list.

Legal Highs

Few parents that I talk to know much about legal highs but they play a major role in the adolescent drug scene. According to a report produced by the Centre for Social Justice in September 2013, the number of Psychoactive Substances (NPSs) or legal highs, now outnumbers classified drugs and a new NPS emerges every week. 'Legal highs' produce similar effects to illegal drugs such as cannabis, cocaine and ecstasy. Unlike their illegal counterparts legal highs are easy to get hold of on the high street or via the internet and they are extremely cheap making them available and affordable to most teenagers. Many teens are nervous about the idea of buying drugs from a dealer but if you can get them legally over the internet they must be ok, right?

It is so important that we talk to our teens about 'legal highs' because, as the report showed, at least one in every 12 teenagers has tried a NPS and the number of deaths linked to use of NPSs has risen by 80% in the past two years.

We need to get the message across to teens that a drug may be legal but that does not make it safe. In 2012 the previously 'legal highs', Black Mamba and Mexxy were made Class B drugs, temporary bans were put on Benzofury and NBOMe in June 2013. The government is proactive but, there is no way it is going to be able to keep up with the ever increasing number of NPSs so talking to your teenagers and getting them thinking is vital:

Where do you think these drugs come from?

Who do you think makes them?

Why do you think they are so cheap?

If someone you didn't know walked up to you in the street and offered you a pill would you take it?

If some previously legal drugs are now illegal do you think there might be others out there that shouldn't be legal?

If fitting in with this group of friends means taking drugs do you think it is the right group for you?

What do you think the implications of taking drugs might be on your family?

We need to educate them so that if they are offered 'a pill' their parrot will be shouting a loud and clear "NO! - you don't know what is in that; you don't know where it came from; you don't know what it could do to you; do not touch it!"

Other online drugs to be aware of

I have just read the tragic story of an eighteen year old student who had finished his A Levels and was on his way to university. He was a promising rugby player, popular and good looking. He died after taking a fat burning diet pill that he had bought online. This pill contained DNP which was originally launched as a slimming aid in the 1930's but was banned five years later because of its damaging side effects. DNP is now used in pesticides and food dye but it is illegal to sell it for human consumption. That said, as I write, it is still widely available online and can be obtained for just £2.20 per 200mg capsule.

We need to be aware that our teens are constantly assessing themselves in terms of how they look. They lack the maturity to appreciate their finer points such as their great sense of humour or good empathy skills, they just want to fit in. In our body image obsessed culture that might mean turning to the internet for quick fix slimming aids, sports performance drugs and other supplements. Talking to them about the danger of unregulated online drugs is important but it is also important to talk about positive body image. We tend to think of girls as being particularly vulnerable in this area but increasingly boys are struggling as they aspire to look like their sporting or media heroes.

Illegal Highs

I hope it is fair to say that for the majority of teenagers heroin is not going to be a problem and so I have limited my exploration of illegal drugs to Cannabis, Ecstasy, GHB, Ketamine and Cocaine.

Cannabis - pot, spliff, grass, weed, reefer, skunk, boom, bhang, dope, draw, ganja, hash, herb, marijuana, puff, resin, sensi, sensemilla, kif and chronic .... is the most accessible and often used illegal drug amongst teenagers. Many of the parents I meet in the workshops think that "smoking a bit of pot" is a rite of passage and not a big deal. The trouble is that the nature of marijuana has changed over the past thirty years leading to a rise in the levels of Tetrahydrocannabinol (THC), which is the main mind altering property of marijuana. Marijuana use has been linked to a range of mental health problems such as psychosis, depression and anxiety and this is only going to get worse if the levels of THC continue to rise.

It is also important to note that although using cannabis does not always lead to use of harder drugs very few people who abuse harder drugs did not start with cannabis.

Ecstasy - pills, XTC, mistubishis, hug drug, crystal, cowies, brownies and MDMA.... has a reputation for being the clubbers' drug as it is used to feel energised and happy and to help them dance for hours. The main problem with Ecstasy is that the active ingredient MDMA is mixed with any number of other drugs so there is no way of knowing what is in it and therefore how it might affect you. Ecstasy causes a raise of body temperature and increased heart rate. It is very unpredictable and kills approximately 27 people per year in the UK some of whom have used it successfully in the past.

I have just returned from a weekend in Edinburgh where it was freshers week for all the new university students. Walking up Cockburn Street we passed Support 2000, an organisation offering advice on drugs. Perhaps because it was the start of the new university term and the nightclubs were packed they had decided to use their shop window to put up information on Ecstasy with the heading "How to use it safely if you are determined to use it".

It read : "Only take half a pill and don't take any more for at least two hours. Be aware that Ecstasy might be mixed with other drugs such as PMA which is stronger, longer lasting and more dangerous. Take regular breaks if dancing and replace fluids by drinking water but no more than one pint per hour. Avoid mixing Ecstasy with downers especially alcohol which can dull the effects of the Ecstasy and make you more prone to dehydration."

GHB - is sold as ecstasy in liquid form and it makes you feel happy, sensual and uninhibited in small doses. The trouble is that the difference between a happy dose and a lethal one is barely noticeable and it is particularly lethal when mixed with alcohol.

Ketamine - vitamin K, super K, special K, K, donkey dust, green...

Ketamine is a powerful anaesthetic most often used by vets to aneasthetise horses for an operation. It is one of the most popular drugs on the party scene despite being banned as a recreational drug in 2006 and reclassified as a Class C drug. There is a groundswell of support amongst the medical profession for reclassifying the drug again because of the bladder damage it causes. There are young people in their twenties whose Ketamine abuse means that they will be reliant on a catheter for the rest of their lives because they have had to have their bladders removed.

Cocaine - white, wash, toot, stones, snow, rocks, percy, pebbles, crack, coke, ching and charlie... cocaine is a powerful stimulant and another popular party drug that gives users a feeling of confidence, energy and euphoria. It can be smoked or snorted; it is highly addictive; expensive and dangerous as it raises the body's temperature and heart rate and can cause convulsions and heart attacks. The "high" is short lived (snorted cocaine takes 20-30 minutes to peak) but the after effects can last days with symptoms similar to a dose of the flu. If there are underlying mental health issues these can be brought to the surface by cocaine.

In conclusion teenagers need to realise that no drug is "safe" and some are highly addictive. They can cause a variety of unpleasant effects and many are just downright dangerous.

TOP TIP *If I am talking to teenagers about drugs I will always finish with this:*

"I cannot be sitting like a parrot on your shoulder saying don't do this and don't take that. You are going to have to make your own decisions but before you even think about taking any form of drug I want you to consider one question and it is this: Are you prepared for today to be the last day that you ever think, feel and behave as you have always done? Because in some people, some drugs can cause life long mental health problems such as psychosis or schizophrenia and you won't know until it is too late whether you are one of the lucky or the unlucky ones?"

Chapter 9
PARROTS ON PARTIES, FESTIVALS AND FAKE ID

YOU MAY FIND YOURSELF FEELING NOSTALGIC FOR THE STICKY MESS OF fairy cakes and musical bumps as you head into the unnerving zone of teenage parties and gatherings (a gathering = less than twenty of your inner circle of friends; party = unlimited numbers and may include friends of friends (plus ones) who you may not know). Horror stories abound with tales of trashed houses, police, stomach pumps and promiscuity but these tend to happen where there has been limited or inadequate parental involvement and they hit the headlines of local newspapers because they are unusual. Take heart, teenage parties can go well, provided they are well planned and there are some boundaries in place.

This said, as they move from being dependent children at ten to independent adults at twenty the time of maximum split, when they swing between the two, is fifteen. It is the time of maximum thrill seeking versus minimum sense so if there is one party to avoid a fifteenth birthday party could be it. Of course, this is when they are most likely to want one as the lure of the peer group grows ever stronger - aargh! If you bow to pressure and agree to an event mid-teens, then at least go for a gathering rather than a full blown party. There is a lot to be said for damage limitation!

Here are some guidelines that I have put together with the help of parents and teachers to make a party a successful occasion:

Parties should be by invitation only and be wary of allowing +1's as it can easily lead to numbers becoming out of control.

Most teens will send invites via a social networking site which is fine provided they ensure that the invitation is only visible to the friends they want to come.

The invitation needs to state a clear start and finish time and give the contact details of the adult responsible for supervision during the party.

Parties should always be supervised by a team of adults who will be in the near vicinity or at the party itself. They

need to be there throughout because whilst they are on your patch they are your responsibility.

Hosts should have a list of telephone numbers of the parents or guardians whose children will be at the party. In case of emergency you need to be able to contact them and you might choose to contact them if their teens' behaviour is causing trouble or angst.

If you serve or provide alcohol for Under 18's (who are not your children) you must have their parents' permission. This can be verbal. If they get drunk on your watch you may be liable for any resulting problems. Interestingly, at twelve, thirteen and fourteen most teenagers, when asked, would prefer to go to a party where there is no alcohol because they feel safer. If it is not available then they can relax and get on with enjoying themselves. Reassuringly most parents, when asked, would not offer alcohol to this age group but please do not be so naive as to think that there aren't parents out there who would. Good parrot training, as discussed in Chapter 7, can help to mitigate this problem.

Most parents I meet think that when their teenagers first hit the party circuit they should contact the parents hosting a party to check that it is going to be managed appropriately. Unfortunately, many don't make that call and it is often because they lose confidence when faced with the horrified reaction of their teenagers "You are so controlling, no one else's parents ring! Don't you trust me?". Doing the right thing for our teenagers is not always going to win us the popularity vote but, we are their parents not their friends and this is an issue of safety. Listen, empathise, reel out the 'elastic' conversation detailed in Chapter 5 but do not budge. As they get older and prove that they can handle themselves at parties then you can start to back off.

If you are hosting a party be aware that some teenagers will try and smuggle alcohol in. I have heard all kinds of sneaky tricks and you have to admire them for their ingenuity. Here are a few - vodka filled water bottles; wrapping bottles up as presents to open later in the evening; hiding bottles in the hedge outside your property to be retrieved later; filling a mouthwash bottle with vodka and a splash of green food dye and, most ingenious of all, filling armbands up with vodka for a beach party - you name it they've tried it. Tell your teens to warn their friends that you will be checking bags. The idea of checking bags feels wrong to many parents but teenagers are used to it and are not fazed.

If you decide to provide alcohol, stick to beer, wine and alcopops unless you are going to make your own cocktails and can therefore limit the quantity of spirits included. Some parents employ devious tactics to limit alcohol intake. They serve alcoholic drinks in jugs and switch to non/low alcohol beer mid evening or water alcoholic drinks down. The problem with this is that, ultimately, it does not teach teenagers to drink responsibly. In fact it might lull them into a false sense of security thinking they can handle more than they actually can.

Serve drinks from a bar that is run either by you or by someone you really trust. Employing older siblings or teenagers is rarely a good plan as they tend to have a few themselves and then become overly generous.

To avoid gatecrashers at bigger parties make sure you have a list of people attending and then give them a paper tyvek wristband as they arrive. They are cheap and easy to buy on line (see Useful Resources) and if you go for a bright colour it is easy to spot anyone without one.

And finally on parties

One of my nephews recently lost his licence for drink driving. We were all very shocked as he adored driving and rarely drank so that he could be the designated driver. It emerged that the party had been a really good one and he decided he wanted to have a few drinks. He talked to the friends he was giving a lift too and they were happy to camp overnight so he drank. At some point he felt tired and went out to sleep in the car but soon after he must have awoken and decided to drive home because the next thing he remembered was hitting the back of a parked car a few miles from the party. Fortunately no one was hurt.

I recounted this tale to a workshop group and suggested that to avoid a drunken change of mind it might be a good idea to tell young drivers to hand their keys over to their hostess. One of the fathers present commented that he had been to parties like that!

Festivals

As I mentioned in Chapter 1, festivals have become incredibly popular and most teenagers will want to attend one sooner or later and the current trend seems to be going with a gang of friends after GCSE's. Many parents feel utterly terrified at the idea of letting their sixteen year old go to a festival but I think festivals offer a relatively safe environment for a teenager to test out his or her independence. Festivals are big business and the organisers would be fools indeed if they failed to pay careful attention to the safety as well as the enjoyment of their customers. The big festivals are extremely well staffed and policed; they will not allow festival goers to bring their own alcohol on site; they will not serve alcohol to under 18's at their bars; there is excellent first aid support on site and they constantly patrol all areas to spot trouble early. In many ways festival sites are safer than your average UK city centre on a Saturday night.

However, if you have been cajoled into agreeing to let them go and are now feeling decidedly nervous here are some tips:

Beware of purchasing expensive festival tickets from anywhere but the official website. Some people have been caught out by scammers who sell them wristbands as an entry ticket. Most festivals issue tickets and only issue wristbands at the entrance gates.

Encourage them to go with a group of friends and take the bare minimum with them eg sleeping bag, sleeping mat, a torch, a few extra clothes, a towel, a toothbrush, wallet and phone.

Encourage them not to take expensive phones, cameras, sunglasses and wallets - cheap pay as you go phones are a good option and get them to programme in the numbers they might need before they go. If they absolutely have to take expensive items then get them to register them on line at www.immobilise.com.

Because of the vast number of phones on site it can be difficult to get a signal so plan for no contact i.e. if you are picking them up after the festival arrange a place and time in advance.

There will be pickpockets at festivals. To make life difficult for them, buy laniards to attach important items more securely. For example, buy a cheap velcro wallet, punch a hole in one corner of it and attach it to a laniard or keyring to make it more difficult for someone to steal it. A small keyring torch is a good idea to help them find their way back to their tent in the dark. Encourage them to put all valuables in their sleeping bag with them when they sleep as it makes them much more difficult to steal.

Encourage them to arrive at the festival well before it gets dark so that they have time to set up their tents and familiarise themselves with the site.

Getting to the front of the crowd to watch their favourite band is tempting to most teenagers but it can also be dangerous if it gets so packed that there is

a crowd collapse or they feel unwell. This can happen anywhere in a large crowd but the area by the stage is a particular hotspot. The security pit teams are good at getting people out but they are not miracle workers so encourage them to think carefully before pushing to the front.

These are things that you can do before they go to a festival but ultimately they need to be able to keep themselves safe on site so start early with the parrot programming:

"if you lose your wallet or phone what are you going to do?"

"festivals are huge - how will you be able to find your way back to your tent?"

"if you decide to buy drugs be aware that there will be undercover police. Drugs are difficult to get into the venue so there is a high chance that what you think is the genuine article may well be nothing more than a vitamin pill."

"it is safer for you to stay with your friends. What will you do if you get separated?"

"if something does go wrong what could you do?' Most of the big festivals will have a security office, first aid and an information

office. It is a good idea to know where they are from the outset so that they know where to go should problems arise.

"you need to look after yourself at a festival. If it is hot it is easy to get dehydrated - drink plenty of water because it would be a shame to ruin your weekend with a bad headache and eat at least one proper meal a day"

"there may be stalls offering tattoos and piercings - you need to be able to keep tattoos and piercings really clean to avoid infection so a festival is probably not the best place to get them done."

"your body is your responsibility - how will you keep yourself safe?"

The UK festival scene is well managed and regulated and festivals have an excellent safety record - if you get your teenagers well organised and programme their parrots there is absolutely no reason why they shouldn't have a wonderful time.

Fake ID

The Home Office Guidance on False ID issued in July 2012 states that under the Identity Documents Act of 2010 "a person commits an offence to have, without reasonable excuse, in his or her possession a false identity document or an identity document which relates to another person." The maximum sentence, if found guilty, is two years or a fine (or both).

It also states under the the Fraud Act of 2006 that "A person commits a fraud by false representation if he dishonestly makes a false representation and intends, by making the representation, to make a gain for himself. Therefore the use of false ID by a person aged under eighteen to obtain alcohol may be an offence under Section 6 of this act." The maximum sentence, if found guilty, is ten years in prison or a fine (or both).

It is relatively easy to get fake ID in the UK. I have met parents who have helped their teenagers obtain fake ID cards and I know plenty of teenagers who have sourced them independently. I think it is important that both parents and teens recognise that not only is carrying fake ID classed as a serious offence but, it also puts teenagers at risk because they may be exposed to people and situations that they are not mature enough to handle

Chapter 10
AND FINALLY

AND SO WE COME TO THE FINAL CHAPTER

We have looked at the developmental drive of adolescence which is to find their identity and autonomy. We have looked at the physical, emotional and cognitive changes that occur and we have considered how these changes drive their behavior. We have looked at our role as parents and how, through effective parrot programming, we can negotiate the fine line between keeping our teens safe and helping them become adults who are ready for the adult world.

Parrot programming for teenagers needs to be age appropriate, factual and measured. Some parents tell their teenagers horror stories of what can happen but I don't believe in the shock tactic approach for two reasons. Firstly because teenagers believe that they are omnipotent so whatever you say won't apply to them. Secondly, when we use scare tactics we undermine our credibility for the next time we want to stock their parrot up with useful information. We tend to resort to drama and shock tactics when we feel unsafe or scared so parrot programming is best done in calm moments.

At the start of adolescence we have a lot of parrot programming to do, but, as the years roll on and they gradually take more and more responsibility for themselves and their lives we should be able to take a step back and let them get on with it.

Parrot programming is all about setting teenagers up to be safe and successful and it can be useful for pretty much any situation:

Cars

The day your teenager either passes their driving test and wants to drive their friends around or wishes to go as a passenger, is an alarming one for any parent. A DfT spokesman said: "Young drivers drive around 5% of all the miles driven in Britain, but are involved in about 20% of the crashes where someone is killed or seriously injured." According to Stephen Glaister, director of the RAC, "young people are four times more likely to die as a result of a road accident than as a result of drink or drugs". The government is looking at measures to reduce the risk that young drivers pose and these might include raising the age at which they can start driving to 18; making 100 hours of supervised driving (20 of these to be at night) a prerequisite to applying for a driving test; enforcing a "no passengers under the age of 30" law for the first year of post qualifying driving. However these are measures that might become law meanwhile how do we help young drivers and their passengers to stay safe?

As parents I think it is vital that we get the message across to driving instructors that we are more interested in them becoming safe drivers than obtaining a driving licence in the shortest possible time. I have met parents who have crammed their teenagers through three lessons a week so that they passed their test within two months of turning seventeen. I appreciate that having an extra driver in the house is useful but all the evidence points to lack of experience and peer pressure being the main causes of young drivers crashing. The more supervised hours driving in all conditions they can get in before they take their test the better. The rest is, once again, down to parrot programming:

If you were a passenger and felt unsafe how could you ask the driver to stop? (remember, it takes confidence to say "you are going too fast" it might be easier to say "I feel sick please slow down/stop."

As you know seat belts save lives - what would you do if, as a passenger, you couldn't find a seat belt for your seat?

If you suspected your driver had been drinking or taking drugs what would you do?

Did you know that drug driving is treated in the same way as drunk driving ie it is illegal?

Why do you think speed limits are important?

How do you think you might feel if you killed one of your passengers because you were trying to be cool and going too fast?

Wo you want the responsibility of driving your friends when statistically one fifth of all new drivers will have a serious accident in the first year of driving?

We need to get them thinking because being in control of a 1200kg lump of metal is serious business especially when they are programmed to take risk, they think they are immortal, they may be trying to impress their friends and they have little driving experience.

Public Transport

Once we have shown them how to use public transport we need to cover the what ifs:

What would you do if you got off at the wrong station or missed your stop?

What could you do if someone harassed you on a train or bus?

What would you do if you lost your ticket?

Do you know how to read a train or bus timetable?

Do you know how to find the right bus stop or platform?

Can you find your way round the London Underground or an airport?

Street Savvy

How will you keep your wallet/purse/mobile safe?

Get your door keys ready to use before you reach the house so you can get in quickly.

How many of you will be in your group and what will you do if you get separated from them?

What would you do if someone stole your bag/wallet/purse/mobile?

What could you do if you were worried someone was following you?

Is your chosen route safe at night or do you need to use a different route in the dark?

Firsts of all kinds

Have you planned how you are going to get there and how long it will take?

Do you think you will be the only person feeling nervous?

What kind of first impression do you want to make?

If you wear those clothes what kind of message are you sending out?

If you are worried about something who could you turn to for support/help?

Let's do the reality checking - do you really think they are going to expect you to be able to do... (a hill start/a philosophy essay/read a spreadsheet) on your first day?

Why do you think they arrange an induction programme/freshers week and what do you want to get out of it?

What is the worst thing that could happen?

What is the best thing that could happen?

How could you help yourself feel less anxious?

What preparation do you need to do in advance?

Are there any practical skills you need to brush up on?

What questions do you need/are you going to ask?

Parrot programming helps teenagers to feel prepared and gives them a greater sense of choice and control which, in turn, increases their confidence.

When we set them up with a well informed parrot we connect with them; we show an interest in their world; we give them our time and empathy, our engagement and energy. If loving is doing then parrot programming is loving. It is not always easy or comfortable or even particularly well received but if we persevere we give them the message that we think they are worth the effort and if we think they are worth it perhaps they will feel the same about themselves.

Life changes and throws up new and interesting dilemmas. As I write, the latest Grand Theft Auto game is due for release and parents are worried about the explicit nature of its content; another teenager has died after taking Ecstasy; schools warn that many of the jobs our kids will do don't currently exist; GCSE's are changing yet again and we question whether a university education is worth the cost or not.

Parenting teenagers in the 21st Century is certainly challenging and like our forefathers before us, I imagine we will always worry about our teens. However, I truly believe that a well programmed parrot is one of the greatest gifts we can give our teenagers because it is adaptable and requires them to think. In short it is that little voice of reason and conscience that will help them to stay safe and do the right thing for themselves and for others.

I hope that this book has given you useful knowledge, an occasional smile and the confidence to talk to your teens. If it helps, think of it as a little parrot programming of your own - a resource that you can call on whenever parenting teens feels too tough and your confidence wobbles, parenting is a marathon not a sprint and sometimes we all need a little help.

And here is my final gift - if you think your teenager is a nightmare at home but wonderful in any other company you have a Street Angel, House Devil. If they can turn it on for other people then you have done a good job so, give yourself a large pat on the back and be patient as you help them to weather the stormy waters of adolescence.

Useful Resources

On-line safety advice for all generations

www.thefamilyfriendlynet.com Ellen Ferguson provides expert digital safety advice through her interactive and practical workshops.

www.thinkuknow.co.uk - CEOP (Child Exploitation and Online Protection) have produced this website giving the latest information on sites, mobiles, new technology, how to use the internet safely and what to do if things go wrong.

www.saferinternet.org.uk - a great website with practical advice and "how to" sections for parents and teens.

On-line guide to downloading

www.childnet.com/resources/downloading/home

A really useful guide to downloading legally and safely from the web. Gives details of legal music, TV and film services.

Resources and reporting bodies for misuse of internet

www.thatsnotcool.com

A good place for teenagers who are unhappy about what is happening to them on line.

www.iwf.org.uk

The Internet Watch Foundation exists for us to report images of child abuse so that they can be removed.

Sexting

www.oiimysize.com - a youth-led project to raise awareness about how boys talk to girls and what is appropriate - get your teenagers to take a look.

Drug Information and Advice

www.drinkaware.co.uk

Lots of facts about alcohol and suggestions on how to talk to children about drinking.

www.teens.drugabuse.gov - An excellent source of information for teenagers and parents.

www.talktofrank - Gives an A-Z of drugs, their appearance and effects, health risks and the law.

Paper Wristbands

www.wristbands.co.uk/wristbands-tyvek - good selection of wristbands for party and event security.

Festivals

www.immobilise.com - this is the UK's national property register. Items registered will be reunited with their owner if they end up in police hands.

Acknowledgements

I would like to thank Vicky Merison and George Elwes for volunteering to be my readers - without their support I am not sure this would ever have been finished. Thanks too to Karen Skidmore whose wise words of wisdom made the whole process manageable and to Ellen Ferguson and Alex Fryer for so generously sharing their knowledge. Thanks to Dominic Latham-Koenig for guiding me through the design and production process and to Sally Valentine for being the most wonderful mentor and role model. To Tim and Annie, my eternal gratitude - it is a wonderful gift to know you are loved. And lastly, but by no means least, to Ben, Eliza and Daisy for their belief, encouragement, patience and humour - did I ever tell you......?!

This book covers some of the content of the Let's Talk Teens Workshop for Parents and below is a snapshot of some of the feedback

"*Really helpful tips and ideas for getting through the teenage years in a resourceful and light-hearted way.*" S Witter

"*Good course content – reinforced general good practice but also gave much needed background to technique. A good opportunity to learn how to turn the negative into positive.*" J Walkinton, Individual Needs Coordinator

"*Honest, down to earth, relevant and thought provoking.*" C Maude

"*If a parenting course can shed the image of 'only-for-problem-families', this workshop does it. Alicia combines up-to-date and thought-provoking information with hands-on advice and practical tips on everything one needs to know about this age group.*" S Deverell

"*Should be compulsory for all parents BEFORE their children become teenagers! Could have saved myself a lot of angst!*" K Healy

"*So many nuggets of wisdom and practical solutions, thank you.*" A Maclean

"If you want to be reassured that you're not alone with the trials and tribulations of teenagers, Alicia will do it. A no-nonsense, positive approach – refreshingly human!" A Boothby

"Alicia's exercises and real life examples are powerful tools in equipping parents with the skills upon which supportive, positive relationships can be achieved. The workshop is outcome focused in terms of how as parents we can promote the development of happy, confident, resourceful and respectful independent adults." Dr SK Agnew; Consultant Clinical Psychologist (Let's Talk Teens Workshop)

"I feel as if I've been given a toolkit to work with – I just have to learn to use it! The course was full of common sense ideas which I can see myself trying to use. I ended up with a clear view of my role as a parent of a teenager and feel better equipped to do that." L Witt

"Alicia is great because she imparts her knowledge in such a relaxed way and uses her own family as examples. Her honesty was very welcome and entertaining." K Pickett

"Any workshop which leaves you with all your questions answered by the end is indeed a rare find, particularly when it is tackling the thorny subject of teenagers!" S Kernon

About the author

Alicia Drummond is a psychotherapist, a parent coach, mother of two teenagers, lecturer, and blogger. Her work brings together the latest scientific and psychological research to help parents to raise happy, confident and emotionally intelligent 21st Century Teenagers.